GINGER SPICE
IN MY POCKET

GERI

SMITHMARK

Photographs: All Action – front & back cover, 1, 3, 13, 14, 17, 18, 21, 28, 31, 32, 33, 34, 39, 40, 43, 44, 48 Capital Pictures – 4, 6, 11, 22, 24 & 25, 27, 38 Retna – endpapers, 9, 36, 47

This edition published in 1997 by SMITHMARK Publishers, a division of U.S. Media Holdings, Inc., 115 West 18th Street, New York, NY 10011.

SMITHMARK books are available for bulk purchase for sales promotion and premium use. For details write or call the manager of special sales, SMITHMARK Publishers, 115 West 18th Street, New York, NY 10011.

Design by Blackjacks

Concept by Clare Hulton

ISBN 0-7651-9128-8

Printed in Singapore

1 0 9 8 7 6 5 4 3 2 1

Library of Congress CIP

Neither the members of the Spice Girls nor any of their representatives have had any involvement with this book.

Full name: Geri Estelle Halliwell

Date of birth: 6 August 1972

**Distinguishing marks:
Two tattoos – one is of a
black panther on the base
of her spine**

Height: 5ft 1in

GERI SPENT HER EARLY SHOW BIZ CAREER IN SPAIN AS A NIGHT-CLUB DANCER AND SHE EVEN WORKED AS A HOSTESS ON A TURKISH GAME SHOW

GERI HAS ALSO WORKED AS AN AEROBICS TEACHER, BARMAID AND CLEANER

WHEN THE SPICE GIRLS DID THEIR COMIC RELIEF NUMBER GERI WAS SPOOKED BY HOW MUCH JENNIFER SAUNDERS LOOKED LIKE HER

GINGER SPICE WANTS BRYAN ADAMS, "COS THE ONLY THING THAT'LL LOOK GOOD ON HIM IS ME.' SHE ACTUALLY MET HIM AND SLAPPED HIS BUM. SHE ALSO PINCHED PRINCE CHARLES' BOTTOM WHEN SHE MET HIM!

WHEN GERI AND MEL B WERE ON HOLIDAY IN SRI LANKA THEY HANDCUFFED A NIGHT-CLUB OWNER TO A TREE TO PREVENT HIM FROM CLOSING THE CLUB AT MIDNIGHT

GERI'S A REAL SOFTY AT HEART — THE FILMS 'DEAD MAN WALKING' AND 'A TIME TO KILL' BOTH MADE HER WEEP

'MY FAVOURITE WORD IS "EXISTENTIALISM". I CAN'T SAY IT AND I'M NOT QUITE SURE WHAT IT MEANS.'

DURING A VIDEO SHOOT GINGER SPICE HAD TO GO TO CASUALTY TO HAVE A FALSE FINGERNAIL REMOVED - FROM INSIDE HER EAR

MEL B SAYS THAT GERI IS GOOD FOR A CHAT.

'IT'S VERY EASY TO GET INTO CONVERSATION WITH HER... BUT SHE CAN BE TOO OPINIONATED ABOUT THINGS.'

GERI'S IDEAL MAN MUST BE FUNNY AND COOL

GERI LOVES TO DRESS UP — SHE ONCE TURNED UP FOR WORK WEARING A NIGHTIE

'SOMEBODY STOLE ALL MY RUBBISH! I CAME OUT OF MY HOUSE TO SEE ALL THESE KIDS RUNNING AROUND. THEN I NOTICED THAT MY RUBBISH WAS GONE!'

GERI SAID THAT SHE DIDN'T CRY WHEN SHE HAD HER TATTOOS DONE BECAUSE GIRLS ARE STRONGER THAN BOYS!

GINGER SPICE CLAIMS TO BE THE BOSSIEST MEMBER OF THE GROUP

GERI MADE HER
BROTHER CRY BY
THROWING A STONE
AT HIM. IT HIT HIM IN
THE EYE AND GAVE HIM
A NOSE BLEED

GINGER SPICE HAD A CAKE FIGHT WITH SOMEBODY ON LIVE FRENCH TV!

GERI ONCE OWNED A FIAT UNO WHICH SHE CRASHED SEVEN TIMES IN SIX MONTHS

GINGER SPICE SAYS THAT YOU CAN'T BEAT ATTITUDE, INTELLIGENCE AND A WONDERBRA: IT'S A LETHAL COMBINATION!